THE TUTOR

Allan Havis

BROADWAY PLAY PUBLISHING INC
224 E 62nd St, NY, NY 10065
www.broadwayplaypub.com
info@broadwayplaypub.com

THE TUTOR
© Copyright 2008 by Allan Havis

1st printing: Dec 2008; 2nd printing: Nov 2011
I S B N: 978-0-88145-407-9

Book design: Marie Donovan
Word processing: Microsoft Word
Typographic controls: Ventura Publisher
Typeface: Palatino
Printed and bound in the U S A

THE TUTOR was first produced by Vox Nova Theater Company (Artistic Director, Ruff Yeager), opening on 4 June 2008. The cast and creative contributors were:

SETH KANE . . . . Mike Sears
ORSON BENTLEY . . . . Josh Adams
MADELINE BENTLEY . . . . Julia Fulton
GEORGE BENTLEY . . . . Fred Harlow

Director . . . . Ruff Yeager
Lighting design . . . . Jason Bieber
Set design . . . . Stan Cole
Sound design . . . . Josh Adams
Production stage manager . . . . Tareena Wimbish

CHARACTERS & SETTING

SETH KANE, *teacher and tutor, mid-forties, personable*
ORSON BENTLEY, *sixteen year old, sullen, wealthy delinquent*
MADELINE BENTLEY, ORSON's *attractive, well educated mother*
GEORGE BENTLEY, ORSON's remote, self-involved father

Time and place: a coastal town in Southern California, 2006

Fourteen scenes over five weeks

In memory of theater artists Chris Parry,
Christopher Markle, Caris Corfman, Floyd Gaffney
and video artist Patti Rabbit

Scene One

(Living room of BENTLEY *home in an affluent neighborhood)*

KANE: Hi? Hello? Can you please take off your iPod? *(Mimes taking off the headphones)* Thank you. I know your Mom lets you smoke, but I have asthma.

*(*ORSON *puts out his cigarette.)*

KANE: Good. Excellent. Wonderful. I read some of your homework assignments and I have a few ideas how we can make the most of our sessions. And I work very fast so you'll see results before the Superbowl. *(Strained smile)* Money-back guarantee. Good. Excellent. *(Pause)* You express yourself with strong, declamatory sentences. I like that a lot. Your verbs are well chosen and, at your best, your journalistic phrases echo a very young Hemingway and your sarcasm reminds me of Hunter Thompson. I'm trying to compliment you, Orson. Do you not like praise? *(Pause)* You know, when Thompson was just out of diapers, he worked for *Time* magazine for fifty dollars a week. Half a century ago. He typed out *The Great Gatsby* and *A Farewell To Arms* as a way to copy the styles of Fitzgerald and Hemingway. That same year Time dumped him for being a snot nose. *(Pause)* You mother told me you have a cold.

ORSON: What?

KANE: She said you're not feeling well.

ORSON: Ahuh. Fever blisters.

KANE: We'll make it a short session today.

ORSON: What?

KANE: Are you deaf?

ORSON: Fuck no.

KANE: We'll make it a short session.

ORSON: Whatever. You know I have a pet snake.

KANE: Fascinating.

ORSON: He's a Ball Python.

KANE: Wonderful.

ORSON: They live a long time up to forty years.

KANE: Good to have a long time friend.

ORSON: Pythons have a reputation as being difficult to feed.

KANE: I've heard that was an urban legend.

ORSON: Sometimes they stop eating for months a time—particularly if they're captive bred. I named him "W" to be patriotic. Almost five feet long. "W" likes T V. He won't eat pre-killed rodents. Fucks up my mother to end.

KANE: Do you know my name, Orson?

ORSON: Mister Cohen.

KANE: Mister Kane.

ORSON: Seth Cohen?

KANE: Seth Kane.

ORSON: Oh, Kane.

KANE: Yes.

ORSON: Like candy cane?

KANE: That's right.

ORSON: Like Caine and Abel?

KANE: Spelled with a K.

ORSON: K as in Kafka?

KANE: People who are sibilant have trouble with my first name.

ORSON: I'm not sibilant.

KANE: I wasn't...

ORSON: Yes, you were...

KANE: Be that as it may, I want you to call me Seth.

ORSON: Seth?

KANE: That's my first name. *(Silence)* Or you can call me Mister Kane. *(Pause)* Or you can just raise your hand... and I'll call on you.

ORSON: Okay, Mister Kane. Seeeeeeeeeeeeeth.

KANE: You probably know I teach at the public school.

ORSON: No, I didn't.

KANE: Well, I do.

ORSON: And that's why you drive a crappy V W.

KANE: Yes, exactly. Mind if I sit down? *(Silence. He sits on the couch.)* I have a bad back. A herniated disc. I tried to move a small fridge one night.

ORSON: A fridge?

KANE: Sometimes I'm not very smart, Orson. Perhaps you watch *Jackass* on M T V? Are you on Ritalin or Concerta? *(Pause)* Hell, it's none of my business.

ORSON: It's none of your business.

KANE: Your Mom alluded to some prescription and I think it's good to know about your meds.

ORSON: I don't take meds.

KANE: Okay. Sorry.

ORSON: Are you on meds?

KANE: No.

ORSON: But she told you I was on some prescription?

KANE: In so many words. In an e-mail. I think I have a print-out...

ORSON: Half the school's on meds.

KANE: I know that.

ORSON: The other half's on diet pills.

KANE: Well, there's some symmetry to that.

ORSON: Did my Mom pick you up?

KANE: No.

ORSON: I didn't see your car outside.

KANE: Your Dad. My car broke down at the Mobil gas station.

ORSON: Big surprise.

KANE: About my car or about your Dad?

ORSON: I hate my Dad.

KANE: All right then. *(Opens a book)* We're going to talk about a few good novels for your English class. I have your class syllabus. And your academic records. *(Pause)* *Gatsby* is a fun book, Orson. It's a witty book. How much of it have you read?

ORSON: What?

KANE: How much have you read?

ORSON: Three pages.

KANE: Good. Which three?

ORSON: The last three. That summed it up for me.

KANE: That's great. You're a speed reader.

ORSON: Ahuh.

KANE: So let's not talk about *Gatsby* today. You can always rent the film if you like Redford.

ORSON: Redford?

KANE: Robert Redford. An actor? Tell me a secret.

ORSON: Why?

KANE: We all keep secrets.

ORSON: That's funny.

KANE: Is it?

ORSON: *(Affects an annoying nerd's voice)* "Tell me a secret."

KANE: That was the name of a party game when I was in college.

ORSON: I detest party games.

KANE: So do I. What turns you on?

ORSON: Nothing.

KANE: Okay. What music do you listen to?

ORSON: Average shit.

KANE: Me too, Orson. Average shit can be so good. 50 Cent or Eminem. Real average shit.

(ORSON *shows his displeasure.*)

KANE: You like Brittany? Fiona Apple? How about rap?

ORSON: Fuck rap.

KANE: Me too. Fuck rap.

ORSON: Fuck you.

KANE: You like metal? Are you a head-banger?

ORSON: Fuck metal.

KANE: Yeah. Me too. Fuck metal. Hip hop? No? I guess you like to fuck jazz?

ORSON: Fuck jazz.

KANE: O K, Orson. Now we're really flying. Let's just see your iPod. *(Reaches for the iPod)*

ORSON: Rule number one. You never touch me. Got it? I don't care who are you or what they're paying you. You never touch me!

KANE: Sorry.

ORSON: What kind of jackass are you?

KANE: I'm not a jackass, Orson. And neither are you. I'm your tutor. Your Mom says you have an I Q over a hundred-and-seventy.

ORSON: She was talking about my bowling average.

KANE: I know you have a very high I Q.

ORSON: Get the hell out of my face.

KANE: In a half hour. *(Pause)* Nick Carraway, a young astute Midwesterner, narrates a keenly observed tale about a mysterious, self-made millionaire doomed by self-destructive impulses. What decade are we in?

ORSON: You'll last two days, tops.

KANE: Know that for a fact?

ORSON: Ahuh.

KANE: You're probably right, Orson. And you'll win. You see, I like to teach but I'm not Annie Sullivan.

ORSON: Who the fuck's Annie Sullivan?

KANE: Helen Keller's teacher.

ORSON: Who the fuck's Helen Keller?

KANE: Ask your mother.

ORSON: Are you a fag?

KANE: I won't dignify the question.

ORSON: Are you?

KANE: *(Reluctantly)* No.

ORSON: How do you know?

KANE: I think the matter is self-evident. Don't you?
(Pause) You don't. *(Pause)* Are you?

ORSON: Am I?

KANE: Yes.

ORSON: I don't like fags, *Mister Kane.*

KANE: You don't really mean that. Maybe you're a fag?

ORSON: Fuck yourself. How much is my Dad paying
you?

KANE: I'll tell you when we get to lesson twelve.
And you'll get a certificate then.

ORSON: You dress like a fag.

KANE: Thank you, Orson.

ORSON: I'd never wear beige corduroy and a shirt
like that.

KANE: Beige is the victory color of working class poets.
(Pause) When I come back again I want you to have
read the *first* twenty pages of *Gatsby.* Do I need to write
that down for you?

ORSON: No.

KANE: And I'm going to get to work on your amazing,
positive essay writing skills. *(Hands ORSON a business
card)* Here's my e-mail address. You can also instant
message me. Send me five pages on why the police took
away your driver's license.

ORSON: It was a hit and run and my dad paid off the cops before the evening news. No one died.

KANE: Great first paragraph, Orson. No sarcasm. Honest.

ORSON: I'd rather write on how I screwed up my summer vacation, *Mister Kane.* *(Pause)* Nice business card. Did you print them yourself online for free?

KANE: A good essay begins with smart attitude, Orson. Let's re-define your attitude. *(Pause)* Can we find a provocative paragraph that anticipates the thrust of your cogent argument?

ORSON: I have no attitude.

KANE: ...while at the same time throws off your reader's suspicions. You won't find that advice in E B White's *Elements Of Style.* You look puzzled, Orson. Do you confuse cogent with cosign?

ORSON: It's almost time to feed my snake.

KANE: Oh.

ORSON: I love my snake.

KANE: Your mother says you have a hard cover dictionary in your room. Did you ever open it up?

ORSON: She's lying, *Mister Kane.* There are no books in my room.

KANE: Then I'll bring you a dictionary next week.

ORSON: You like me, don't you?

KANE: I don't really know.

ORSON: But you think you like me?

KANE: Do you want me to like you?

ORSON: Not if you're a world class fag.

KANE: *(Laughs in spite of himself)* Thank you, Orson.

ORSON: That's a stupid laugh. Do you think Mel Gibson is a jerk?

KANE: I don't know.

ORSON: Are you into Mayan ruins?

KANE: Not really.

ORSON: Do you think Jesus enjoyed torture?

KANE: No one enjoys torture.

ORSON: Some pussies like it, don't you think? You know his *Mad Max* films?

KANE: I do.

ORSON: If you turn off the sound to *Road Warrior* and play Metallica's second album, it's a perfect head film.

KANE: I try that tonight when I get home.

ORSON: Do you think he wants all the Jews in the world to die or just the ugly ones?

KANE: Very hard question to answer, Orson.

(ORSON's mother, MRS BENTLEY, enters.)

MRS BENTLEY: How is everything going?

KANE: Absolutely fine.

MRS BENTLEY: *(Berating* ORSON*)* Stop making fun of the Jews, darling. This is the decade of tolerance. *(Pause)* Would you like some coffee or a cold drink?

KANE: No, I think this should be a short visit today.

MRS BENTLEY: Was Orson attentive?

KANE: Very.

MRS BENTLEY: *(Smiling)* You needn't be a diplomat, Mister Kane.

KANE: I come from a family of dysfunctional, charming diplomats, Mrs Bentley.

MRS BENTLEY: Is that right?

KANE: My father worked at the U N.

ORSON: With a fucking white, bushy moustache?

KANE: ...and my grandfather was stationed at various embassies in Europe.

MRS BENTLEY: Then how is it that you ended up at public school?

KANE: For five years I taught at a four year private college, but I'm a firm believer in excellent public school education—if society will ever heal as one.

MRS BENTLEY: Society will never heal because of the highly organized Christian right wing nuts. And my neighbor is one of the biggest Christian pricks in California. Do you need a ride home?

KANE: Yes.

MRS BENTLEY: I hate driving. And seat belts. Did I ever mention that?

KANE: No.

MRS BENTLEY: I think cars are like coffins with a due date. What if I just phone a cab?

KANE: That's fine.

(ORSON's cell phone rings.)

ORSON: It's motherfucker Tucker. This guy rocks! *(He exits without excusing himself.)*

MRS BENTLEY: His friend Tucker is a terrible influence. You know what I mean. Last month the two of them pulled a horrible prank on their high school principal, Doctor Emmit. They placed seven A M yard sale notices in every newspaper in the city and dumped a truckload of junk on Emmit's front lawn. It was the morning of Emmit's daughter's wedding. *(She makes a "tsk tsk tsk"*

sound.) We refuse to have Tucker come by to visit
Orson. Riff raff of the worst sort. Orson got head lice
from him. Lice eggs ruin cashmere sweaters, Mister
Kane. And I love cashmere. Word is that Tucker
poisoned a child last Halloween with D-CON rodent
pellets but no one has any proof. *(Pause)* You look upset.

KANE: Do I?

MRS BENTLEY: As if your pet dog died.

KANE: I don't have a pet.

MRS BENTLEY: Would you like a drink?

KANE: No, thanks.

MRS BENTLEY: Mind if I do? It's after six and, sober,
I can't stomach the evening news on T V.

*(KANE says nothing, and MRS BENTLEY pours a drink from
the living room bar.)*

MRS BENTLEY: My husband TiVos Jon Stewart to
impress Orson, but Orson hates the show. Did my
husband say you are to get paid by the day or by
the month?

KANE: He didn't say.

MRS BENTLEY: What would you prefer?

KANE: By the month is fine.

MRS BENTLEY: That shows confidence.

KANE: How do you mean?

MRS BENTLEY: Expecting to last a month.

KANE: I believe in long term gratification.

MRS BENTLEY: I don't.

KANE: I'm a very good tutor.

MRS BENTLEY: I'm a very good wife. Sounds like
two very transparent lies.

KANE: Mrs Bentley...

MRS BENTLEY: I'm trying to be funny.

KANE: Oh...

MRS BENTLEY: You're not so certain, Mister Kane.

KANE: About what?

MRS BENTLEY: About contemporary humor. And that's today's lesson. You need the right tools to reach Orson.

KANE: I would agree.

MRS BENTLEY: If want to reach him before he reaches you, Mister Kane. Trust me on that.
You settled on the dollar amount?

KANE: Yes.

MRS BENTLEY: Did my husband bargain you down?

KANE: Yes.

MRS BENTLEY: He prides himself about squeezing people on fixed salaries.

KANE: I sensed that.

MRS BENTLEY: Why did you take on this job?

KANE: For the opportunity.

MRS BENTLEY: What opportunity?

KANE: Teaching troubled teens is always an opportunity.

MRS BENTLEY: That's the boring, generic answer, unless you're Sidney Poitier.

KANE: I am Sidney Poitier.

MRS BENTLEY: *To Sir With Lust*? At any rate, Orson's been through about nine home study teachers.

KANE: Your husband gave me all the sordid details.

MRS BENTLEY: Good.

KANE: Let's give it time with your son, Mrs Bentley.

MRS BENTLEY: Orson really would have excelled had he been a girl.

KANE: What makes you say that?

MRS BENTLEY: A bitchy girl is a piece of cake.

KANE: But he's your son.

MRS BENTLEY: I'm not convinced. Gender is not sex.

KANE: And sex is not always gender.

MRS BENTLEY: I hope you get through to my son.

KANE: Time will tell.

MRS BENTLEY: He's a good boy on legal holidays.

KANE: Yes. I'll keep that thought.

MRS BENTLEY: You can see intimate things from a distance. Listen to the things teens say and do. Or you can simply tune out the horror.

KANE: Well put, Mrs Bentley.

MRS BENTLEY: When I'm mildly delusional, I think he's turned a corner.

KANE: That's what your husband said.

MRS BENTLEY: That I'm delusional?

KANE: Your husband thought Orson's about to turn a corner.

MRS BENTLEY: Then we all agree?

KANE: Every teen should turn a corner, Mrs Bentley.

MRS BENTLEY: I blame the hormones, Mister Kane.

KANE: So do I, Mrs Bentley.

MRS BENTLEY: The miserable hormones from a
miserable God in a faraway heaven. What sort of
father are you?

(End of scene)

Scene Two

(The next day)

MR BENTLEY: I know I've made probably too many
mistakes. My father was never there for me, I was
determined to be unlike my father. There's no such
thing as a social disease. I think we all need to know
that and feel good about that. Look at me, Orson.
When you avoid my eyes I feel awful. I love you dearly.
Disease is a state of mind and a kind of personal hell.
There is no social disease because disease is not social.
(Pause) I was always afraid of high altitudes, cold
rooms, and extreme situations. Many close business
friends told me it had to do with my anxiety about
losing a small fortune in stocks. And maybe they were
rivals and not friends? Hearing that I had two choices,
Orson, and neither choice was comfortable—I had to
take longer business trips. So again, I reminded myself
there is no such thing as a social disease. The last
thing I want to know about myself is the poverty of
imagination and my cowardice. So I pushed ahead and
pretended that we came from a powerful line of men.
Orson, put down your cell phone. Thank you. *(Pause)*
It's all about that hard to define notion called male
power. How simple everything in life becomes once
you see the lines. Up and down. Side to side. Almost
self-evident. In the material world we see two clear
examples of real power. Horizontal. Vertical. Up and
down. The visible, empirical, unmistakable realm of
masculine power is Vertical. Generals of armies employ
Vertical power. C E Os thrive on Vertical power.

Professional athletes. Lions in the jungle. You get my drift, don't you? But side to side, what is that really? Horizontal power is found, first, in nature's camouflage—to work we have to be fooled. Deception is the key advantage here. And with it, the element of surprise. Water eroding a massive stone ridge at Yosemite. A Venus flytrap. Quicksand. Lady Macbeth controlling her husband. All becomes the act of deception. A poison chalice is horizontal. A steel sword is direct. The chalice won't caution you, but the sword telegraphs everything. Young men need to know that you have to respect both realms of power even if we all come to respect the forward face of the sword. *(Pause)* I lost a lot of money recently in glamour I P Os and I fired my broker when I realized he was getting points under the table. It happened to be monies coming out of your trust fund, Orson. Let this be instructive even if I say so. *(Pause)* Your mother told me you went to get a tattoo over the weekend. You know I don't like tattoos. They're terribly juvenile and inoffensive.

ORSON: It's smaller than a dollar bill.

MR BENTLEY: Look at me, Orson.

ORSON: No. I didn't get anything pierced, Dad.

MR BENTLEY: Orson.

ORSON: What?

MR BENTLEY: Don't piss me off. Do you understand? Answer me?

ORSON: Okay, Dad.

MR BENTLEY: Do you understand?

ORSON: Yes.

MR BENTLEY: Your mother and I are about to separate. It's a trial separation. And I really hate trials. You shouldn't be surprised. This hell has been going on

for months. Your mother and I are struggling to find
harmony and to restore the magic we once had. I can't
go on in life without a little magic. *(Pause)* There's
a little woman at my office, Orson, that has grown
excessively attached to me. Like me, she suffers from
psoriasis. Don't laugh. She works very hard and has
a degree from Vassar. We had dinner on several
occasions. Little Phyllis. This is not easy to talk about,
but you deserve the truth. I feel loved by this little
woman. She's just a few years older than you, Orson.
That makes things stranger to comprehend and I tried
very hard to be professional and mature. She had
a medical scare two weeks ago and broke down in
my office. Phyllis thought she had ovarian cancer.
It turned out to be a benign cyst. I lost all sense of
myself and drove her home. She made me come into
her apartment. One thing led to another, son, and you
know at core I'm a very religious man. We give each
other deep comfort and that feeling is impossible
to ignore. *(Pause)* Are you listening to me, Orson?
I won't repeat this.

ORSON: That she's little?

(MR BENTLEY *smacks* ORSON.)

MR BENTLEY: I told your Mom what had happened.
She was not shocked or annoyed. She seemed to know
things before I even got there. Her facial muscles
relaxed for the first time in many years. She forgave me
and asked me to take time with choices. Those were her
words. Take time with choices. She said I should talk
to you as soon as possible. The worst thing that could
happen, according to your Mother, would be for the
rumors to get to you before I got to you. I want you to
be strong about this news and to know, when I move
out of the house next month, that I will still be here for
you.

(End of scene)

Scene Three

(A few days later)

MRS BENTLEY: Vice President Cheney's daughter is pregnant. Isn't that something? She's not married. No. No. No. And I wonder what Ellen DeGeneres will say to soften Rosie O'Donnell's political jokes. The Cheney family must have paid quite a small fortune for her privacy at the fertility clinic, don't you think? Whom do you think the father is? Sasha Baron Cohen? You don't follow pop culture, Mister Kane?

KANE: Not as much as I should.

MRS BENTLEY: All of contemporary life can be seen through Ellen's eyes or darling Rosie's. There's nothing really left in the middle. *(Pause)* My husband goes out of town on business more than he has to and I think that has added to Orson's off color moods.

KANE: You know when Orson has these moods?

MRS BENTLEY: Yes, I asked an astrologer to graph them at the beginning of each month. It's Orson's version of P M S.

KANE: Thank you for telling me.

MRS BENTLEY: You could have guessed as much. My husband and I did have an amazing honeymoon that lasted for countless hours, but one learns in business that a lavish honeymoon is no different from a corporate signing bonus. Are you married, Mister Kane?

KANE: Divorced.

MRS BENTLEY: You still wear a ring.

KANE: I gained weight. I'd have to cut it off.

MRS BENTLEY: I'm sorry.

KANE: So am I. She got the house.

MRS BENTLEY: And you got the wedding album.

KANE: Yes.

MRS BENTLEY: We have two copies of our wedding album—as part of the pre-nuptial.

KANE: Where's Orson?

MRS BENTLEY: Orson? He called from urgent care. There was a minor accident. He dislocated his shoulder with his idiotic friend who has a black belt in judo. Doesn't the Russian President have a black belt in judo? At any rate, his friend took him to the hospital. They're just finishing up.

KANE: You have no other children?

MRS BENTLEY: My husband has a teen daughter by a former marriage. She lives in Michigan and stays with us during the summer months. Not a perfect arrangement. She's a militant lesbian. Do you have children, Mister Kane? I seem to ask you this question a lot.

KANE: I told you when we first met. *(Pause)* Two daughters. My wife and I have joint custody.

MRS BENTLEY: Not a perfect arrangement.

KANE: You know Orson keeps a lot of gun magazines under his bed.

MRS BENTLEY: Yes, it was either that or the damn pornography. His father prefers that he stay away from things with high sexual content.

KANE: Does he keep a gun in his room?

MRS BENTLEY: George does, yes.

KANE: But does Orson?

MRS BENTLEY: I would hope not.

KANE: Guns scare me, Mrs Bentley.

MRS BENTLEY: Good for you, Mister Kane.

KANE: Do you ever search his room?

MRS BENTLEY: God, not! He keeps a pet snake.

KANE: This is still your house, Mrs Bentley.

MRS BENTLEY: Was that a car door?

KANE: I didn't hear anything.

MRS BENTLEY: What a loud, awful sound. I think my husband's back. *(Looks out the window)* It's the police.

KANE: Really?

MRS BENTLEY: And all the neighbors take notice. Damn them all. We had a break-in yesterday and they wanted to come back for a little more information. Thieves got into my jewelry and my husband's gun collection— including his high ballistics from Germany. Quite a nice assortment of goodies, don't you think?

KANE: That's quite serious.

MRS BENTLEY: We think it was someone from Orson's high school.

KANE: What makes you say that?

MRS BENTLEY: Orson told me. A gang of teen girls in cheerleading clothes. The school's newsletter reported we're in a major crime wave and the authorities think our kids are hording guns.

(KANE goes to the window.)

MRS BENTLEY: You walk with a slight limp, Mister Kane. Are you all right?

KANE: Bone spur. The cops are just sitting in the car.

MRS BENTLEY: That's fine by me.

KANE: Moody kids and guns don't mix. I'm concerned about your son.

MRS BENTLEY: For years I was pleased by him and it hurts me so today. He used to talk to me all the time about everything. When he was happy or sad. When he was stung by a yellow jack. When he lost his first tooth. When he had his first wet dream. And he was only ten. I knew it was right to breastfeed him until he was walking. And walking upright took forever. Were you breastfed?

KANE: I don't remember.

MRS BENTLEY: If all children were breastfed I really believe there would be no wars on earth.

KANE: You may be right. It's an interesting theory.

MRS BENTLEY: It's more than a theory. Orson's a virgin, Mister Kane.

KANE: Many kids are.

MRS BENTLEY: He's afraid of girls. Are you?

KANE: No.

MRS BENTLEY: Orson thinks girls will steal his imagination and his seed. Were you afraid of losing your seed at his age?

KANE: No.

MRS BENTLEY: I know you have an imagination, Mister Kane.

KANE: I do.

MRS BENTLEY: Orson used to recite this poem to me every night—
Teenage girls
In ribbons and bows
Teenage girls
Old Grandpa knows

Beautiful girls.
Short ones.
Tall ones.
Fat ones.
Thin ones.
Girls never perspire.
They glisten.
Debs love to sing
They never tire.
(Pause)
Isn't that by Ogdon Nash?

KANE: I don't know.

MRS BENTLEY: You don't like Ogdon Nash?

KANE: I didn't say that.

MRS BENTLEY: Are you related to Ogdon Nash?

KANE: No.

MRS BENTLEY: What a stupid question! *(Pause)* Let's get
away from the window. Cops hate to be watched. You
know my husband had climbed Mount Everest last
spring. He spent over sixty-five thousand dollars to
reach the summit. Never asked me if I would object.

KANE: Did you?

MRS BENTLEY: *(She laughs.)* He trained for three months.
I told him that 1 out of eleven assholes die at Everest.
"What's death?" said hubby. George loved the odds
because he's an asshole. His life insurance strictly
forbade extreme sports like sky diving and Vegas
orgies. Had George died, no payment to the
beneficiaries. Worse, Orson was really upset like
an infant wetting his bed at night—wicked dreams
about Everest. George bundled his vacation time—
independent of us—to make this his own little triumph.
He read *Into Thin Air*—you know, books on tape—and
was obsessed like a pimpled face boy scout. My mother

told me to file for divorce, but George met his goal. He
reached the summit under ideal conditions. Dumb luck.
All this became his bragging rights even though George
was one of the forty guys who passed a dying British
climber. David Sharp. It was in the newspapers, of
course. "Dilettantes from a dozen countries and their
underpaid sherpas turn their back to Brit climber!"
I screamed at George when he told me the news, but
all he said was that's the mountain code. "You focus
on your goal. Period." *(Pause)* Like Orson, I had a lot of
weird dreams when George was away. I really believed
he was going to die a horrible death or come home
crippled. And if truth be told, I wanted him to come
back a paraplegic. Did you ever see that film *Breaking
The Waves* with Emily Watson? *(Pause)* Since he came
back from Everest, George feels totally invincible.

KANE: Maybe you wanted him to die?

MRS BENTLEY: For one brief moment I did want that.
And I talked to God about my negativity. God forgave
me, Mister Kane. We are defined by our negativity,
never by our positivism. It's funny, I get a lot of
speeding tickets and I ask the traffic cops to forgive
me but they never do. Christ, do you have to go down
a highway patrol officer to get a break? Are you dating?

KANE: No.

MRS BENTLEY: Do you hate the word?

KANE: No

MRS BENTLEY: But you avoid dating?

KANE: No.

MRS BENTLEY: Do you think divorced people are
allowed to date?

KANE: Yes.

MRS BENTLEY: Do you think the Catholic Church invented the missionary position?

(KANE *fakes a smile.*)

MRS BENTLEY: Getting words out of you is like pulling teeth.

KANE: My ex-wife is a dentist.

MRS BENTLEY: When I was a teenager I thought sustained oral sex meant having an affair with one's orthodontist. If you were George, would you have let a man die on the top of a mountain?

KANE: Is that what really happened to your husband?

MRS BENTLEY: Yes. Would you pass a man who was dying atop a killer mountain?

KANE: I have vertigo, Mrs Bentley. But no, I wouldn't pass a dying man.

MRS BENTLEY: Orson thinks you're gay.

KANE: I'm not.

MRS BENTLEY: I know that.

KANE: I'm not even a metrosexual.

MRS BENTLEY: I think Orson's very attracted to you.

KANE: I hope not.

MRS BENTLEY: You probably conform to some fantasy figure in a graphic novel. I love the word—graphic. Do you? You make him laugh, Mister Kane. He believes you have a natural irreverence.

KANE: At times, yes. Is that good or bad?

MRS BENTLEY: We all need a good laugh.

KANE: Do I make you laugh, Mrs Bentley?

MRS BENTLEY: *(Suppressing a laugh)* No. But you amuse
me in a quiet way and for that I find you endearing.
And I stopped noticing men years ago.

KANE: Can you tell me something about Orson's hit
and run?

MRS BENTLEY: George must have filled you in. It was
quite a scandal.

KANE: And?

MRS BENTLEY: Orson was lucky. He nearly killed a
homeless man at a city intersection.

KANE: Was he high?

MRS BENTLEY: Does it matter?

KANE: I think so.

MRS BENTLEY: Orson is wired differently from other
boys. Maybe he's just like his father. Neither George
nor Orson have any sense of remorse about their
actions. They only believe in luck. You would think
they have stones in their heart. They must be reptilian.
And as a result they don't feel deep hurts of others.
But they damn know the distinction between right and
wrong. They know how to argue for the underdog. And
they always win. If they are wrong, they make it right.
Because words are full of tricks. I don't expect you to
instruct Orson on ethics and moral behavior, because
you might as well teach a monkey to sing. Well,
actually I saw a monkey sing on Animal Planet cable
and I was very impressed. Is this all crazy talk? I must
be very lonely, Mister Kane. And that's worse than
ovarian cancer. *(Back at the window)* Maybe the city
police are working for George. George's always buying
cops drinks and dinners at this tawdry strip club
downtown. What's it called— "Sugar Tits Sally"?
He's too cheap to hire a private detective, even if it's
tax deductible. And when George's drunk, he's

unbearable jealous. Of course, George thinks I'm
sleeping with you at Motel Six. High style adultery.
And what the hell can I say about that?

(End of scene)

Scene Four

(Next week. On the living sofa and companion arm chair)

ORSON: Do you hate coming here?

KANE: Not at all.

ORSON: Are those reading glasses?

KANE: Yes.

ORSON: Do you like my mother's perfume today?

KANE: I didn't notice.

ORSON: She uses an industrial size applicator for those
hard to reach spots.

KANE: I've a sinus infection, Orson.

ORSON: You know women watch as much porn as men
do.

KANE: Gee whiz.

ORSON: It's in a national study. More men buy it, more
women rent it. And the Jesuits can't get enough of it.
(Pause) Did you ever shoplift when you were my age?
(Pause) Gus Van Sant just got busted for D U I. Bet you
the blood work will show a little recreational drug
action. When ever I get blood work done, the lab just
tells me I've anemia.

KANE: Do you get a lot of blood work?

ORSON: I can metabolize antifreeze, Mister Kane.
(Pause) Did you see Van Sant's film *Elephant*?

KANE: Yes. On a little screen.

ORSON: I didn't like it much. I was waiting for the fucking elephant to show up. *(Coming very close to* KANE*)* You tell me a truthful answer and I will too. Okay?

KANE: Okay.

ORSON: Did my mother try her brilliant moves on you?

KANE: What?

ORSON: Only the truth.

KANE: It's a rude question.

ORSON: Those are the rules.

KANE: You're not in the position to be making rules, Orson. *(Pause)* No she didn't.

ORSON: She will.

KANE: Thank you for telling me.

ORSON: She doesn't care if you're a fag or not.

KANE: What have you against homosexuals?

ORSON: Well, for one—fags have more like sex than rabbits.

KANE: What have you against rabbits?

ORSON: Big floppy ears.

KANE: Is that the only reason?

ORSON: Fags are arrogant.

KANE: And you're not?

ORSON: Fags like parades and pink banners. And they strut around with a stick up their ass. Now you get to ask me a tough question even though you lied.

KANE: I didn't lie.

ORSON: I've seen my mother in action. *(Sharp impersonation of his mother's voice and body language)* "Maybe the city police are working for George. George's always buying cops drinks and dinners at this tawdry strip club downtown. What's it called— "Sugar Tits Sally"?

KANE: Very good, Orson. You're a natural thespian.

ORSON: She has these lamebrain fantasies about day laborers coming to our house and servicing her on the billiard table while Janet Jackson sings. She used to listen to old Janis Joplin shit, but I threw away all her C Ds. Go ahead. Ask me a question.

KANE: Do you have remorse for the hit and run accident?

ORSON: Honest answer?

KANE: Honesty is the best policy.

ORSON: No remorse. I never learned how to cry, Mister Kane. Crying is a lost art and I hope to master it. A good cry can burn up some calories. Crying without a twinge of guilt. Do you ever cry?

KANE: I read your essay, Orson.

ORSON: Did you like it?

KANE: Not much, but I grew to like the writing.

ORSON: No shit?

KANE: There's a sense of elevated circumspection in your literary voice. Different on the page than off.

ORSON: Are you saying that I'm an erudite asshole?

KANE: Yes and you use a good many active and yet unfamiliar verbs...

ORSON: Like exculpate?

KANE: ...and these verbs add bounce to your perverse thoughts.

ORSON: You realize that I wrote a proper paper on abortions, anal sex, and stem cell research.

KANE: Yes, if proper means grammatically allowable possibilities on your views of sodomy.

ORSON: Sodomy sounds like a brand name. Like Marlboro, Nike, and Thinkpad. I would market Sodomy as a cologne or game board for the Aspen crowd.

KANE: It's clear to me that you're not a feminist.

ORSON: Oh?

KANE: And not pro-choice.

ORSON: And you are?

KANE: Yes.

ORSON: A feminist?

KANE: Pro-choice.

ORSON: Every dickhead should wear a two dollar condom.

KANE: You're absolutely right. And there a lot of dickheads out there.

ORSON: We agree!

KANE: You know Nancy Reagan came out in support of stem cell research.

ORSON: *(Flip)* But not the Pope and certainly not *the Dolly Parton.*

KANE: I like the Dixie Chicks.

ORSON: So does "W" —my snake. Mistakes cost lives.

KANE: That's clearly your message.

ORSON: S T Ds are no joke. My Dad has genital warts that landed on his fucking face. I'll never kiss him again. And AIDS can jack you up like no mother can.

KANE: Know anyone with AIDS?

ORSON: No. Do you?

KANE: Yes. It's no boast.

ORSON: Sounds like you're boasting.

KANE: Horrible to witness a slow death.

ORSON: Didn't Camus say that?

KANE: Maybe he did but that's not on your syllabus.

ORSON: My syllabus?

KANE: Did you like *Gatsby*?

(ORSON *shrugs*)

KANE: You read the entire book?

ORSON: Yeah. Honest. Fitzgerald is as facile as Gore Vidal.

KANE: What do you read for fun?

ORSON: Albert Camus. Camus' biography in French. A little Jean Paul Sartre—*Sartre never washed himself and smelled like a hog.* Underground political journals. Soldier of Fortune. Aryan Nation. Shit like that. And Popular Mechanics to keep my idle hands busy.

KANE: You like building things?

ORSON: Painless mousetraps, rooftop solar heaters and elegant pipe bombs that are biodegradable.

KANE: I don't always know when you're pulling my chain.

ORSON: You'll know when I yank, Mister Kane. I like Robin Hood more than the Unibomber. Like Geraldo more than Che Guevara. Like Martha Stewart more

than Angelina Jolie—because Martha's lips are natural.
You never know with me. I must be counterintuitive.
I used to make runs into Tijuana and return with a
trunk load of wetbacks. I did it for fun. Never charged
a cent. Never got caught. *(Laughs)* My friend Tucker
is the dangerous fuck. He's like Timothy McVeigh and
Charles Manson rolled into a messy enchilada. I'm just
fucking guacamole next to him.

KANE: Is that a picture of Tucker in your room?

ORSON: You were in my room? *(Pause)* Yeah. He's got
a slack jaw and a little eye shadow to hide the albino
element. The motherfucker's white as a ghost. Albinos
were in with Edgar Winter, but then came *The Da Vinci
Code.* I read that book on acid and was ready to take on
the Opus Dei bare handed. Did you ever drop acid?

KANE: A few times.

ORSON: No shit?

KANE: It was a phase. Angel Island in San Francisco Bay
before John Lennon was shot.

ORSON: Did you like tripping?

KANE: Yes.

ORSON: I would have never guessed.

KANE: There was a helpful book by Humphrey
Osmond.

ORSON: What about Huxley's *Doors Of Perception*?

KANE: Good book.

ORSON: Did you know Huxley dropped acid on his
death bed?

KANE: Yes.

ORSON: It was November 22, 1963. The day Kennedy
was killed.

KANE: Fascinating. Does Tucker have a picture of you in his room?

ORSON: I don't know. I'm not allowed to visit his room.

KANE: Why is that?

ORSON: House rule. Can't break it.

KANE: Are his parents strict?

ORSON: Yes.

KANE: Is he a Nazi?

ORSON: No. Nazis love backdoor sex. Why ask that?

KANE: He dresses like a Nazi.

ORSON: So did Prince Harry, the anus-wart of Wales.

KANE: You have a way with words.

ORSON: Thank you, Mister Kane. We'd be maggots without words.

KANE: Are you upset about your father?

ORSON: When you bite your lower lip, you remind me of Robin Williams in *Good Will Hunting*.

KANE: I often feel like Robin Williams in *Popeye*.

ORSON: Did he make *Popeye*?

KANE: Let's get back to your Dad.

ORSON: Fuck Dad. He thinks I'll go into his business.

KANE: Many fathers have that fantasy. My father owned a restaurant.

ORSON: What sort of restaurant?

KANE: A Jewish deli in New York.

ORSON: I'll kill myself before I become my father's stooge.

KANE: You'll never become a stooge. That's for certain. Is Tucker's a bad influence?

ORSON: Yes, so what?

KANE: I heard about Tucker from your parents.

ORSON: What shit did you hear?

KANE: He was suspended last year.

ORSON: That was because of our 'Vatican' school dress code.

KANE: He brought a gun to the cafeteria.

ORSON: It was a fake gun that shot out a banner of Pamela Anderson. And he wore a Z Z Top beard and we were all pissing in our pants.

KANE: Still, he had nearly everyone fall under the cafeteria tables.

ORSON: Fuck, it was on April Fools Day.

KANE: Does Tucker sell dope?

ORSON: Hell, he gives dope out for free. Now that's a high school hero. Do you think Tom Cruise will pop out of the closet?

KANE: You guys are playing with real guns.

ORSON: Do you think Richard Gere had a gerbil up his ass? Or was it just a motorized toy? How did that rumor hit the streets?

KANE: Are you guys playing with fire arms?

ORSON: What are you, a cop?

KANE: No.

ORSON: Then keep your Jewish nose out of my life.

KANE: Your e-mail messages are whacked out. I got one meant for Tucker.

ORSON: Oh, they're pretend games. Just for fun.
Like fantasy baseball.

KANE: What do you mean?

ORSON: Tucker wrote a cool short story in MySpace.
About the murder of Alexis Trachenberg. Really had
great style and rhythm. A bio-chem death in the high
school science lab. Did a great job in PhotoShop with
the illustrations. Tucker thought it cool to attack every
Trachenberg orifice with a toxic substance. And she got
sick the next week after he posted the story. You see,
Tucker really likes Dario Argento films. Italian
Hitchcock with a twisted touch.

KANE: I know Argento - he's a follower of Mario Bava's
films.

ORSON: Bava's *Black Sunday* is too cool, man. But
you could really appreciate this if you knew Alexis.
She's such a cow. Like no other mad cow in the world.
She walks around top heavy like she's carrying three
bazooka tits. And she's got this dumb Jewish smile
that drives me insane. You know the face, on the dumb
balloon cartoons at the mall, and that backside of hers
that is bigger than a fuck-ass Hummer. Tucker tried to
mount her once, but he couldn't get hard to save his
life. My Dad can't stand Tucker and I kind of love that.
My Mom lets Tucker come to the house just to piss
off my Dad. I kind of love that too. She lets us get
high if it's the weekend. So you got to give her credit
sometimes. I'd love to get high with you, Mister Kane,
but that shouldn't surprise you. My Mom is an only
child, you see. And that's why she needs to be part
of the scene. We both want you intensely.

(End of scene)

Scene Five

(ORSON's *first monologue*)

ORSON: Happy birthday, Daddy. I remembered. Only inside my little boy scout diary. Here's something for you. I want you to open it. Yeah, and the card's inside. How old is the old man today? Okay. I don't need to know your age. But I think you're a fag, Daddy. And you have a wide stance at the urinal and at the toilet stall. I notice these things because I've got a sharp eye. *(Pause)* My gift to you? A silk blouse from Nordstrom's. Couple of hundred bucks. Yep. That's all Mom talked about last week. An imported blouse from Italy. But she was in on you. It's your favorite color, Daddy. Robin's egg blue. And you know I'm color blind. *(Pause)* I know you've embezzled a shitload of money from the corporation. Maybe the cops will never know because you know how to play the cops. And I know little Phyllis has you eating from a doggy bowl. And Mom is a million times superior to this little cunt Phyllis. And I know Jesus is smiling down on us right now 'cause Jesus knows I am capable of doing great historic deeds. Aren't we all searching for our beautiful reward, Daddy? *(Pause)* Reward and a whisper.

(End of scene)

Scene Six

(The next week, at the BENTLEY *home)*

ORSON: Did you know that a male Australian redback spider courts a female for hours and hours and strums the strings of her web?

KANE: No.

ORSON: Think of Orpheus and Eurydice. What a wonderful image. And once the Australian starts to mate, he flips onto her fangs.

KANE: Clearly you're more than a young herpetologist.

ORSON: Do you celebrate Sadie Hawkins Day?

KANE: I don't want to cover a lesson today.

ORSON: So the spider continues after her while she chomps down on him. Sexual cannibalism. The fucking Australian's dead meat.

KANE: Orson...

ORSON: Just like the male praying mantis, Mister Kane. The female takes off his head right after copulation.

KANE: Look at me, Orson....

ORSON: What?

KANE: I spoke with Lucinda Ward last night.

ORSON: Lucinda?

KANE: Yes.

ORSON: You know her?

KANE: Yes.

ORSON: Wow! Did she phone you?

*(*KANE *nods affirmatively.)*

ORSON: She's a pain in the butt.

KANE: Is she your girlfriend?

ORSON: No.

KANE: She said you guys are going out for half a year.

ORSON: Why would she call you? What else did she tell you?

KANE: Stuff she wouldn't tell your folks.

ORSON: Like what?

KANE: That she's pregnant.

ORSON: It's a pretend pregnancy. What else?

KANE: That you are obsessed about Columbine High.

ORSON: She said that?

KANE: And that you feel kinship with Dylan Klebold.

ORSON: I really don't because Klebold was dimmer than a penlight bulb. But I kind of relate to Perry Smith *In Cold Blood*. And you kind of look like Truman Capote when you wear your sun hat and cross your legs.

KANE: What if she's pregnant, Orson?

ORSON: Am I the Daddy? Who's to say? D N A?

KANE: Maybe it will come to that.

ORSON: Maybe you'll come to the baby shower?

KANE: Are you the father of Lucinda's baby?

ORSON: This is why most guys stick to oral sex, Mister Kane. What do you like?

KANE: I asked if you were the father.

ORSON: I appreciate your concern, Mister Kane.

KANE: Are you planning something with Tucker?

ORSON: About Lucinda?

KANE: No, about your high school.

ORSON: If you don't want to cover a lesson, let me be the tutor today. Did you ever read Celine and Michel Houellebecq?

KANE: Some Celine.

ORSON: Both use pen names.

KANE: I know.

ORSON: Who wrote *Journey To The End Of The Night*?

KANE: I know the answer and, Orson, the proper title is: *Voyage Au Bout De La Nuit*.

ORSON: And the time period?

KANE: World War I and the immediate aftermath in France, in Africa, and in the U S.

ORSON: Do you have a problem with Celine?

KANE: Like Joyce, Celine played with the rules of punctuation.

ORSON: That's not it, Mister Kane.

KANE: He was a known anti-Semite.

ORSON: Louis-Ferdinand Celine was a master at describing a personality ripping apart.

KANE: Like Houellebecq?

ORSON: Celine could have been Houellebecq's fucking godfather. You got to read Houellebecq's *The Elementary Particles*.

KANE: Why?

ORSON: It's got two half-brothers—Michel and Bruno. A scientist and a teacher. They were trashed by their parents. Bruno will fuck anything in sight. Michel loses his way as the wiser brother. Snuff films are part of the ride. Both men get a little hope at the story's end—but there's really no hope from up high in my bleacher seats.

KANE: Are you reading these authors in their original language?

ORSON: No. It would take too long, Mister Kane, and you know I like to speed read. Besides a dirty French word sounds hygienic.

KANE: These writers are morally bankrupt, Orson.

ORSON: Like de Sade and Genet?

KANE: No need to limit yourself to the French. There are wonderfully obscene German and Italian authors to savor.

ORSON: For some reason, I like the French.

KANE: Fine. *(Pause)* Are you planning something with Tucker?

ORSON: That again? *(Pause)* No. Yes. I don't know. Why should I tell you?

KANE: I need to know.

ORSON: You don't *need* to know. You're not my fricken chaperon.

KANE: Is it just a prank?

ORSON: Yes, sir. And nothing to lose sleep over.

KANE: When?

ORSON: For Christsakes! A couple of weeks.

KANE: With weapons?

ORSON: With balloons. Water balloons.

KANE: Come on, Orson.

ORSON: Come on—what?

KANE: I'm not fooling around.

ORSON: When I bullshit you, you just get real cunty.
Don't get cunty. I think it's best to stick to the fucking
lesson plan, Mister Kane. Your lesson plan. The great
books of William Faulkner and Ian Fleming. Would
you name your daughter Pussy Galore?

KANE: I don't want you fucking up any students.

ORSON: I won't.

KANE: And I don't want you hurting yourself. I believe
what your girlfriend is saying.

ORSON: Then go fuck her.

KANE: I'll stop this tutorial.

ORSON: And go to the cops? You're dying of curiosity.

KANE: Guns? Pipe bombs?

ORSON: Neither.

KANE: Then what are you planning?

ORSON: A Domino Dilemma. We're going to surprise
the cafeteria with a pre-paid large Domino pizza
delivery. I can't tell you anymore if you're going to
talk to the cops.

KANE: I'm not going to the cops.

ORSON: Scout's honor?

KANE: Scout's honor.

ORSON: Tucker wants to Ex-Lax the school. Everyone
that eats pepperoni and sausage. He's willing to spare
the vegetarians.

KANE: That would be fine, Orson, if I could believe this
was just about laxatives.

ORSON: *(Takes out a hidden wicker basket that will shake
itself in time.* KANE *assumes a snake is inside.)* Is my
mother putting you up to this?

KANE: No.

ORSON: She's not telling you to be Jiminy Cricket?

KANE: Please.

ORSON: No matter how big my nose grows? My nose is growing, Mister Kane. Go ahead and touch it. My nose snakes at night. A proboscis that defies medical science. Touch it, Gepetto. Let me be your pet. *(Laughing)* Snakes are fascinating, and with regular handling can be quite tame, Mister Kane. However, snakes are obviously not for everyone. They have special needs and should only be kept by those with the loving commitment to understand and meet their needs.There are several snakes which can be found as pets—but of course some are more lovable than others. The types range from common garter to huge pythons. But no matter which type of snake, a secure escape-proof enclosure will be essential. Snakes can be quite persistent in trying to get out. So make certain that your enclosure has no gaps, or prepare to become an expert at tracking snakes in your house.

KANE: Am I tracking?

ORSON: Let me give you a few pointers. *(Pause)* Start your search near the cage and go from there. Check behind furniture along the baseboards. Check under the furniture. Check inside cabinets, drawers, shelves and bookcases. Check behind, in, and under any items in these places. Remove cushions from couches and chairs, and check down the sides and back of the furniture. Check the underside of furniture and beds for any holes through which a creature could climb inside the furniture/bed. Check inside any boxes you have around the house, including tissue boxes. Look in boots and bags, or any other small, dark hiding places you can think of. Check the undersides and backs of appliances for holes. Make sure the cage is left open, and place favorite treat or food around and in cage.

KANE: Orson.

ORSON: Place foil around the room in hiding places so you can hear your snake moving around. Sprinkle some flour on the floor in areas where you suspect it might be hiding—you might get a set of footprints to help you. Tips: Don't discount a hiding place because you think it is too small or inaccessible—snakes can fit through surprisingly small spaces. If your pet is nocturnal, consider putting out its favorite treat after dark. *(Pause)* Are you nocturnal, Mister Kane? You have to give others a chance.

(End of scene)

Scene Seven

(A few days later. MR. and MRS BENTLEY are in the living room meeting with KANE.)

MR BENTLEY: Mrs. Bentley will be out of town all next week during Spring Break. Maybe you can keep an eye on Orson for us?

KANE: Certainly.

MR BENTLEY: How many weeks have you been working with Orson?

KANE: Three.

MR BENTLEY: Are you happy with the progress?

KANE: No.

MR BENTLEY: Is there progress?

KANE: Yes, some.

MR BENTLEY: *(To his wife)* Darling, are you aware of any progress with Orson?

MRS BENTLEY: A little bit.

MR BENTLEY: I don't want half answers. Don't insult my intelligence. Please. *(To* KANE*)* I don't find this amusing, Mister Kane.

KANE: It isn't, Mister Bentley.

MR BENTLEY: Is Orson harder than other kids his age?

KANE: He is.

MR BENTLEY: Does it have to do with my role in his life?

KANE: Perhaps.

MR BENTLEY: Do you think another tutor would be better for him?

KANE: I really don't know. That's your choice.

MR BENTLEY: Actually, the choice is my wife's.

MRS BENTLEY: I think the choice is Orson's. Have you talked with your son recently?

MR BENTLEY: Why are we having this meeting, Madeline? Orson's nearly off his probationary period. Everything's just peachy.

MRS BENTLEY: No, George.

MR BENTLEY: You know, it's perfectly okay for him to masturbate during the day.

MRS BENTLEY: That matter never crossed my mind.

MR BENTLEY: At least, he's not getting disciplinary reprimands from his high school these last three weeks.

KANE: Well, that is good news.

MR BENTLEY: He's had other tutors before, Mister Kane. More costly than you.

KANE: Yes, Orson's told me.

MR BENTLEY: Since you've been working with him, Orson's spending less time with this strange boy Tucker. And that's sweet. I don't like this boy at all. Do you know Tucker Smith?

KANE: I've only heard about him.

MR BENTLEY: I met his father, Mister Kane. Roger Smith. He's a top engineer in the Defense Department and he drives a modified Prius. His son is nothing like him. I've had a few conversations with Roger Smith over the phone. And my wife knows his sister, Lily. Isn't that right, darling?

MRS BENTLEY: I don't know what you're talking about.

MR BENTLEY: Madeline, you had her over once when you were presenting for that Breast Cancer Awareness benefit.

MRS BENTLEY: It was Colon Cancer Awareness week.

MR BENTLEY: Lily has that perforated eardrum and reads lips.

MRS BENTLEY: I think you've the wrong woman in mind.

MR BENTLEY: My memory is finer than yours.

MRS BENTLEY: I never met Lily Smith.

MR BENTLEY: She might have a different last name. Maloney? Halstrum? What difference does it make? She has a goddamn perforated eardrum. How many women do you know with a hole in their ear?

MRS BENTLEY: George...

MR BENTLEY: (*To* KANE) Why do you look so unhappy?

KANE: Orson talked about one of the stunts Tucker is planning.

MR BENTLEY: Christ. Don't tell me.

MRS BENTLEY: George...we should know.

KANE: Tucker told your son that he's going to "kidnap" a girl from the school.

MR BENTLEY: "Kidnap"?

KANE: Technically, yes.

MR BENTLEY: The kids are just pulling your leg.

KANE: I don't think so.

MR BENTLEY: Why?

KANE: Because they're scary kids.

MRS BENTLEY: He's right.

KANE: Tucker is determined to terrorize this high school girl. He's planning to force her to a mountain cabin for ten days.

MR BENTLEY: Kidnapping is a federal offense.

KANE: I know that, Mister Bentley.

MR BENTLEY: He's better off just pelting her car with rotten eggs.

MRS BENTLEY: George, don't be an idiot.

KANE: And he's trying to enlist Orson's participation.

MR BENTLEY: That's absurd.

MRS BENTLEY: We should phone the police.

KANE: Yes. Immediately.

MRS BENTLEY: You know the police captain, George. You can make this a discrete thing.

MR BENTLEY: Do you really think this is necessary?

MRS BENTLEY: Yes.

MR BENTLEY: What if this is just a stunt to get us to panic?

MRS BENTLEY: Why gamble?

MR BENTLEY: Why risk embarrassing us?

MRS BENTLEY: Your new girlfriend is turning you

into a world class moron.

MR BENTLEY: Shut up.

MRS BENTLEY: Look at you...

MR BENTLEY: Alright, Madeline. *(Turning to* KANE
You should make the call, Mister Kane. And the police
can ask you everything you know and what to do.
I don't want to get into a personal feud with Tucker's
father when no crime has been committed.

MRS BENTLEY: But you know more, George, about the weapons.

MR BENTLEY: What the hell do I know?

MRS BENTLEY: Tucker and Orson were involved with a lot of awful things in the last 9 months.

MR BENTLEY: Nothing on the scale of kidnapping, Madeline!

MRS BENTLEY: Fine, Seth. I'll call the police,

KANE: And I'll come to headquarters with you.

MR BENTLEY: *(To his wife)* Are you sleeping with him?

MRS BENTLEY: What?

MR BENTLEY: Is my wife sleeping with you?

MRS BENTLEY: What if I am?

MR BENTLEY: I'm talking to him.

KANE: No, Mister Bentley. She's trying to piss you off.

MR BENTLEY: Is that what she's trying to do?

KANE: What the hell do you think?

MR BENTLEY: I'll kill you both without hesitation.

MRS BENTLEY: And who will visit you in prison, darling? My mother? What's really going on, George? You moved out weeks ago. You're living with some bimbo without a brain in her purse.

MR BENTLEY: You're living with Orson. You have to maintain some decorum.

MRS BENTLEY: Decorum?

(ORSON, *with rubber snake, enters in his underwear.*)

MRS BENTLEY: What difference does it make who's in my bed? If this man can teach our son to get out from under Tucker's wicked thumb, I have nothing but admiration for him.

ORSON: Go to hell, Dad.

(ORSON *throws fake snake at his dad, and* MR BENTLEY *reacts awkwardly.*)

(*End of scene*)

Scene Eight

(*A week later. Outside* ORSON's *house*)

KANE: Orson! Open the door! Damn it! It's Seth Kane!

ORSON: (*O S*) Go away!

KANE: You phoned me. Let me in.

ORSON: I shouldn't have phoned you. This is real shit now.

KANE: Let me help you.

ORSON: Tucker's with me.

KANE: Stop lying.

ORSON: Tucker's got a gun!

KANE: Your guns

ORSON: I'm not shittin' you!

KANE: Calm down.

ORSON: Get lost!

KANE: Who else is with you? Is Alexis Trachenberg with you?

ORSON: He'll kill me if he catches me talking to you. He'll be back any minute from the 7-Eleven.

KANE: Is the girl with you?

ORSON: Yes.

KANE: Is she O K?

ORSON: I don't know.

KANE: What do you mean you don't know!

ORSON: Shit.

KANE: Open the damn door, Orson.

ORSON: She's sleeping it off, Mister Kane.

KANE: Did you drug her?

ORSON: Are you alone?

KANE: I'm alone. What did you give her?

(ORSON *unlocks the door and peers out.*)

ORSON: Is that your V W over there?

KANE: Yes.

ORSON: Are the cops coming?

KANE: I'm going to drive her home.

ORSON: That's crazy, man. You'll just piss off Tucker.

KANE: Why did you phone me if you're going to give me a lot of crap?

ORSON: I don't know.

KANE: Let me come in and help you with Alexis.

ORSON: I don't think I can trust you anymore.

KANE: Of course you can. Look. I'll stay outside. Just wake Alexis and bring her to my car.

ORSON: I need to talk to Tucker.

KANE: You don't.

ORSON: He hates if I fuck things up.

KANE: Do as I say, Orson! *(Pause)* Orson, I'm pleading with you.

ORSON: You really impress me, Mister Kane. A lesser man would have called the cops.

KANE: You don't need to screw up your life.

ORSON: You're right.
What are you going to tell Alexis' parents?

KANE: The truth. Give me the gun.

ORSON: Why? You'll only get yourself and all of us in trouble. They'll want a police report.

KANE: Give me the goddamn gun.

ORSON: *(Removing one gun hidden against the back of his trouser belt. He hands it over to* KANE*).* You're so cool. Like my very best friend, Mister Kane. *(He reenters his house and in a few moments returns holding a woman's body wrapped inside a blanket.)*

(End of scene)

Scene Nine

(Later that night at the BENTLEY *home.)*

KANE: I drove Alexis home. Conscious but her speech was sluggish.

MRS BENTLEY: I can't believe these boys anymore.

KANE: Yeah.

MRS BENTLEY: Sit down. You look like a wreck.

KANE: I wasn't acting responsibly but I was trying to protect your son.

MRS BENTLEY: You should have phoned me before you went into action.

KANE: For Christsake, you were in Coronado.

MRS BENTLEY: Catalina.

KANE: Catalina.

MRS BENTLEY: So what happens now?

KANE: I called the police and issued a report about Tucker's guns.

MRS BENTLEY: But not about Alexis?

KANE: No.

MRS BENTLEY: Thank God.

KANE: I threw away Orson's gun.

MRS BENTLEY: Why protect Orson?

KANE: I have to.

MRS BENTLEY: I'll send him to jail.

KANE: You wouldn't do that?

MRS BENTLEY: Watch me.

(End of scene)

Scene Ten

(The next day. Living room)

ORSON: Lucinda gave me an ultimatum—so I chucked the two guns. One—a 9MM Luger, my father gave me for my birthday— "Momsy" doesn't know. The .357 Magnum—I bought at a gun show last summer.

KANE: I'm glad you did. Lucinda has good sense of things. What made you pull away from Tucker?

ORSON: Maybe it was you.

KANE: I got you to change your thinking?

ORSON: I don't know.

KANE: I want you turn in all the firearms to the police.

ORSON: All right, Mister Kane.

KANE: What's going to happen to Lucinda and you?

ORSON: You mean the baby?

KANE: Yes.

ORSON: I'm going to let her have the baby.

KANE: Your mother doesn't know?

ORSON: I plan to name the baby after you. Citizen Kane.

KANE: Orson...

ORSON: Mom told me you called the cops on Tucker. But for some reason, the cops never came to question me. I think my Dad got to them before they were dispatched.

KANE: I covered for you, Orson. I threw your gun away.

ORSON: You did? *(Pause)* Tucker's got a stash of guns
in his school locker. He's going to be hell on wheels
for you and for me. And I don't want you to get hurt.
I really like you. I told everyone that at school. *(Pause)*
I wish Tucker were dead. I really mean it. He scares the
shit out of me. Kids thinks he's in a Satanic cult. Animal
sacrifice, pissing on graves, drinking menstrual blood.
You got to help me.

(End of scene)

Scene Eleven

(The next evening)

KANE: I don't like myself. I probably would inflict harm

if I had any courage. It starts first thing in the morning
at the bathroom mirror. I feel the razor against my neck.
Then I disassociate from my arm. *(Pause)* I was married
for twelve years. The marriage should have flourished.
(Pause) We had three children. Two survived. *(Pause)*
Do you believe in tragic accidents? *(Pause)* I don't.
But we waited a long time for a son. My wife had faith.
She always had faith. She talks to God and God
acknowledges her. That was always her talent.
And I accepted this as sign that God loves most
people who walk the wet earth. *(Pause)* She loves
our daughters in her own way. Twin girls. They were
six years older than our son Eric. *(Pause)* My wife had
worshipped our son. Eric knew that even at an age
when a baby cannot walk. I loved the boy with all my
heart. He was the bonus baby. I never made a great
mistake in my entire life. I was home with our baby
one night when my wife was out with friends. It was
twilight and I was out in the backyard. We have a wood
deck that overlooks the quiet cul-de-sac. The twins
were watching T V inside. A Disney or a Barbie movie,

I think. *Princess And The Pauper*. *(Pause)* The moon was full. I felt lonely that night. No particular reason. But the loneliness was truly piercing and God was nowhere in sight. *(Pause)* I don't know how it happened, but I dropped Eric. He was shifting in my arms and I was not paying attention. I was vacant. Or paralyzed. I reacted too slowly. Eric hit the wood head first. It was a severe concussion. He was in a coma and died three days later. That was God addressing me, you see. I died that week a thousand horrible deaths. I lost my mind that year. I lost my wife. Lost my two daughters. Lost the most precious blessings a man could possibly ever know. Would you call that a biblical event? Or would it be easier to call me a monster?

MRS BENTLEY: I'm so sorry for you.

KANE: I took a leave of absence from work. There was no respite. Except a return to teaching. Winter and summer. Weekdays and weekends.

MRS BENTLEY: I should have guessed something was killing you inside.

KANE: I look at my hands. I look at my hands.

MRS BENTLEY: So you help grown boys, Mister Kane.

KANE: Maybe prison would have been the right ending.

MRS BENTLEY: Prison?

KANE: A right ending is needed, Mrs Bentley.

MRS BENTLEY: Call me Madeline, damn it.

KANE: I can't.

MRS BENTLEY: Then call me Maddy.

KANE: The accident happened in Eugene, Oregon. I moved south.

MRS BENTLEY: No one knows.

KANE: No one knows here.

MRS BENTLEY: Why tell me?

KANE: I don't know.

MRS BENTLEY: Do you trust me that much, Seth?

KANE: No.

MRS BENTLEY: Friendship takes away misery.

KANE: How do you know?

MRS BENTLEY: I read it in the *Reader's Digest.*

KANE: Is there really a *Reader's Digest* anymore?

MRS BENTLEY: Did your wife re-marry?

KANE: Yes.

MRS BENTLEY: How soon?

KANE: Almost immediately.

MRS BENTLEY: I don't believe that.

KANE: Within a year. She married her divorce attorney.

MRS BENTLEY: Do you think you're going to die young?

KANE: No. Why should I get a break?

MRS BENTLEY: I think you deserve a break. I could be wrong. I often am. Fuck it. You deserve even more than that. Look at you. Just look. Sadder than a basset hound and lonelier than a nailed Catholic martyr. You don't know the pleasure of a happy life.

KANE: And you do know?

MRS BENTLEY: I do. And pleasure comes in cycles. Like Halley's Comet. You wait with your hands in your pocket. And you wait. And you needn't wait for me. *(Pause)* I have to tell you something that is a little scary, Seth. It's about Tucker Smith. I went to see him at his home. Maybe I was stupid to make the trip but I couldn't put it off any longer. Tucker is not whom you or I think he is. Not in the slightest. Tucker Smith is a meek little nerd. A mouse. That's all he is. He has coke bottle eyeglasses and a mop haircut. He never owned a gun and he never tormented that Jewish girl in school. Tucker's the president of the school's chess club. Orson built a fabulous masquerade around a silly teenager.

KANE: What?

MRS BENTLEY: *(She hands him a hardcover notebook)* This is Orson's diary. I read it from cover to cover. Everything was a hoax. Take the diary home. Read the entire damn thing. *(Pause)* How could he fool everyone? Orson can do anything for fun. Orson made Tucker into Orson's caricature. Orson is "Tucker". That was my worst fear. He pulled us into a cruel, practical joke. You thought you were successful freeing Orson out of the devil's grip. My son is a demonic actor. I admire his talent.

KANE: I don't.

MRS BENTLEY: Oh, you do. I've seen you showing your approval. I have to tell you something. Orson is in love with you. And he'll do anything to win you completely.

KANE: Why are you telling me this?

MRS BENTLEY: Because I have no one else to talk to. Because I know how much you cry in your sleep. Because we deserve each other. Because I wake up in the middle of the night and wish you would stop my mind from its ugliness. We have all the time in the world to think about our private failures. I could have been a splendid mother. I forgive you, Seth. All of your sins. So reciprocate. Orson will never know why you quit helping him.

KANE: Where is Orson?

MRS BENTLEY: He went to his father's for the weekend.

KANE: Why didn't you tell me earlier?

MRS BENTLEY: The air. The air. The heaviness of my
breathing. The air, Seth.
Orson took a sweater and drove to see his father.
I bleed inside and no one cares.
Sit beside me, just for now.
I can't see my breath.
Hold my hand.
For Orson.
Hold me.
Please.
Maybe he'll kill his father.
We don't seem to take in the same air.
I'd rather have Orson find a way to clean his soul.

(End of scene)

Scene Twelve

(ORSON's second monologue)

ORSON: Hey Mom. I know you're reading this shit.
Let's get married. That's right. You heard right. I'm not
fucking drunk. If we marry, it's not Freudian and it's
not Oedipal. It's simply legal. Where? Las Vegas. I got
a car for a few days. Come on, Mom. I really thought
it over. Fucking Lucinda is no better than singing like
turtledoves at Christmas. And if I'm not good enough
for you, why don't you just snare Kane? He's available.
He's into you. And a notary at the Mailboxes U S A
store can write your next pre-nup. That's karma. *(Pause)*
I'm not in trouble, Mom. I can't write that enough
times. But I'm really worried about your boozing.
It's going to kill you. And I'm all that you have left
in the world. So stop this shit and get on Zero Coke.
And if you clean up, maybe I will clean up. What do

you say to that? I'll leave you a big space on the next page to write your reply.

(End of scene)

Scene Thirteen

(The next day)

ORSON: You don't look happy.

KANE: I'm not.

ORSON: Do you want me to buy you lunch?

KANE: No.

ORSON: How about a drink?

KANE: No.

ORSON: I owe you a lot.

KANE: You owe me nothing.

ORSON: Why did you tell my mother that you're quitting?

KANE: It's time we stopped.

ORSON: Isn't that my decision?

KANE: No.

ORSON: Are you scared?

KANE: Your mother can return the books I've loaned you.

ORSON: I can put everything inside a box if you wait a few minutes.

KANE: I have to go now.

ORSON: You hate me.

KANE: No.

ORSON: Then what's eating you?

KANE: *(From his attaché comes* ORSON's *diary)* Your fucking lies.

ORSON: I don't lie. How the hell did you get my journal!

KANE: Everything about Tucker was total crap, Orson.

ORSON: My writing has nothing to do with the freakin' truth. You said it yourself, Mister Kane. Great artists use writers' conceits—from Shakespeare to Norman Mailer. Jonathan Swift destroyed a physician by writing a fictional obituary. Even a mediocrity like Clifford Irving scammed the invincible Howard Hughes.

*(*KANE *throws the diary at the floor.)*

ORSON: *F Is For Fake*—Orson Welles.

KANE: You could have ruined his life with these stunts.

ORSON: But I didn't.

KANE: The police found five guns in Tucker's school locker.

ORSON: They were birthday gifts.

KANE: They were loaded. He's never been your friend.

ORSON: That's a matter of opinion.

KANE: Everything about Tucker was a hoax.

ORSON: What's your point?

KANE: You invented "evil Tucker".

ORSON: Is that a question?

KANE: Tucker is a good kid.

ORSON: It took you a long time to figure that out.

KANE: I can't believe it took this long to get it.

ORSON: Why don't you give me a big loving hug?

KANE: You're just a fucking little punk.

ORSON: My Mom told me about your baby boy.
I'm so sorry for you, Mister Kane.

KANE: No, she didn't.

ORSON: Yeah, she did. How else could I have known?

KANE: I don't know and I don't give a damn.

ORSON: I know you much better now. I cried when
I heard the story. Really. Goddamn. It's tragedy.

(KANE, *furious, grabs* ORSON'*s shirt collar.*)

ORSON: Now I understand everything.

KANE: I doubt that.

(KANE *pushes* ORSON *away with two hands.*)

ORSON: Are you moving away?

KANE: Yes. Did your mother tell you that also?

ORSON: You're not a coward, Mister Kane. Stay the
course. I'm defending you.

KANE: I don't need your defense.

ORSON: You do. You taught me so much. You know
that. I'm not hell bent to take out the entire school
anymore. I'll never bring guns to school again. I'll never
go postal. Boy Scout's honor! So you have to give me
a chance. Come on, Mister Kane. Stay with me. I need
you.

KANE: No.

ORSON: Please. I won't let you leave me.

KANE: Good bye.

ORSON: And that's a promise.

(*End of scene*)

Scene Fourteen

(One week later. hospital room)

ORSON: Hello, Mister Kane. It's Orson. I'm dreadfully
sorry for you. *(Pause)* I know you can't speak and
the nurse said I could only stay for a few minutes.
I brought you roses. Pink roses. I guess we need a vase
and some water. *(Pause)* I know you you're in a coma
and I found myself praying every night to God to keep
you alive. I felt that God was hearing me out and there
was never a real "busy signal" on the line. I tell kids
at school that I believe in God now. I think I will get
to church and light a candle to show my supplication.
(Pause) I aced my English Lit final. Got the second
highest score in the class. Thanks to you, Mister Kane.
Really. Some things are pure magic. *(Pause)* Can't you
talk just a little? *(Pause)* My Mom and Dad were really
upset to hear what happened to you. Dad really
showed emotion. And you could see a few tears welling
up in his eye. *(Pause)* Tucker stole my snake, Mister
Kane. He had my house key and the alarm code.
I thought he would never take my pet. He knew my
snake was my best friend. He killed my snake. *(Pause)*
Everyone underestimates Tucker because people think
I'm the killer. I wouldn't harm a fly. My mother taught
me to hold back from that sort of thing. I thought
Tucker would only do stunts to scare me. Because
I taught him everything I know and he picked up
everything like a sponge. But *he* put the fucking rattler
inside your car. I don't own a rattler. That motherfucker
bought a rattler in T J. Now Tucker knows how bad this
turned out. He's like Ed Norton in *Primary Fear*. You
know, like Jeckle and Hyde. Fooling even the Devil.
(Pause) The nurse said you had complications from
rhabdomyolysis. Man, that is so out. Rattlers never

bothered Eve. Never bothered Adam. They only
bothered God's angels. And really I am to blame for
all of your pain. When I really should say something
I feel in my heart. I love you, Mister Kane. I love you.
I love you. I love you. And fucking Tucker was so
jealous of you that it had to come to this. I was lying
sometimes but you knew when I was honest. I love
you like a father, Mister Kane. I really love you.
I'm so ashamed of how things turned out. And I'm
afraid that I've lost you. A boy needs a father. I need
to be bleached clean, Mister Kane. Please don't abandon
me. I beg you. I would even die for you and burn in
hell. Please give me a chance?

END OF PLAY

www.ingramcontent.com/pod-product-compliance
Lightning Source LLC
Chambersburg PA
CBHW052223090426
42741CB00010B/2655